# OUTER SPACE HUMOR

*Compiled by Charles Winick*

*Illustrated by James Schwering*

*The Peter Pauper Press*

*Mount Vernon, New York*

# TO THE READER

*Life on other planets has been a subject of discussion for thousands of years. Recently, flying saucers and Sputnik have served to arouse Americans to the realistic possibility of travel between planets. This possibility, enhanced by the successes of our astronauts, is so real that it has entered into many jokes that have become part of American folklore.*

*The best of these jokes are set forth in the pages that follow. A few of the stories have been contributed by Mr. Paul Lowney, to whom grateful acknowledgment is made.*

*Whatever their deeper meaning, these Outer Space stories are funny. So, onward and upward!*

CHARLES WINICK

An Earth man landed on the Moon.
His first sight was a Moon man carry-
ing a sign which read: "Repent, the
Moon is coming to an end."

The bulbous Martian had agreed to cooperate with a group of scientists and submit to a physical examination. "We'll examine the eyes one at a time, so I'll just put these little patches of cardboard there, and here, and there, and here..."

♂     ♂     ♂

An odd-looking Venutian played all afternoon at the gaming tables in Las Vegas. But no one noticed him until he made fifteen consecutive passes.

♀     ♀     ♀

The visitor from Uranus had landed near a night club. He heard the band playing and walked in. The drummer was pounding away on the drum. The Uranus visitor approached the drum and asked it solicitously, "Need any help?"

♂     ♂     ♂

An Earth man landed on Pluto and the first thing he saw was a gorgeous 25-foot girl. He went up to her and said: "A ladder now — your leader later."

The man from Mercury landed his space ship outside a jazz club. He stopped someone leaving the club and asked, "Who are you?" "Dad, I'm a cat," replied the jazz fan. The man from Mercury said, "Great! Take me to your litter!"

☿     ☿     ☿

Three Martians landed in New York dressed in Earthling clothing, went into a fancy restaurant and ordered a complete dinner. After dinner, the waiter asked if they were Martians. Completely amazed that he had guessed, the Martians asked the waiter how he knew. "It was easy," he explained, "you're the only ones to pay cash for the past month."

♂     ♂     ♂

Two Moon men walked up to a parked car, and one of them said: "Take me to your leader." There was no answer so he repeated his demand. Still no answer. Enraged, he kicked in a headlight. "Shame on you," said the other Moon man, "hitting a kid with glasses!"

A boy told his father that he had taken a ride on a flying saucer and had been given a pill to transform him into a real Martian. Indulgently, his father told him that his imagination was a bit too wild. Suddenly there was a loud whirring noise in the street and several little green men stepped out of a space ship. "Run, run," the father screamed to his son, "get in the house and lock the door. We're in trouble." "What do you mean, 'WE,', you miserable, weak Earthling," sneered the boy.

♂    ♂    ♂

A strange looking space traveler, in a bright and shiny skin-tight space suit, with rear tubed epaulets, landed in Times Square and went to the information booth. "Take me to Liberace," he said.

♈    ♈    ♈

Two visitors from Venus were watching water skiiers skimming over the top of the lake. One Venutian said to the other: "Inferior equipment. They've been at it all afternoon and not one of them has been able to take off."

The space craft from Jupiter landed in Monaco. A group of natives approached the vehicle and said, as the visitor got out, that they would take him to see their prince. "No, no," exclaimed the visitor. "Take me to your leader's wife."

♃        ♃        ♃

A couple of Venutians, under instructions to bring back two Earthlings, landed, uprooted two gasoline pumps and flew back to Venus. "Well done," said the King of Venus, "now we'll breed them and we'll all have slaves." "Not so fast," said the Court Scientist, "can't you see they've brought back two males?"

♀        ♀        ♀

A visitor from Jupiter, watching a typical Western on television, remarked to a friend: "How come the hero has a biped riding on his back?"

♃        ♃        ♃

Dr. Edward Teller, the father of the hydrogen bomb, was once asked what we'd find on the Moon when we finally got there. He replied: "Russians."

A Moon man asked the bartender for a screwdriver. The bartender served him a drink. "That's awfully nice of you," said the Moon man, "but now may I please have a screwdriver? My head's loose."

☺     ☺     ☺

A man from Neptune saw a wire mesh trash basket on a street corner. "What a shame," he whispered to his friend, "with those flimsy clothes, she'll freeze to death."

♆     ♆     ♆

The Martians were watching a young man inserting quarters into a slot machine. After an hour and a half, his persistence was rewarded. He hit the jackpot and out came a torrent of nickels. "Too bad," said one Martian disapprovingly. "Rich food will do it every time."

♂     ♂     ♂

We may kick about the cost of putting a man into a capsule, but speaking as a man who's bought his share of antibiotics, it's almost as costly to put a capsule into a man!

Several Martians landed in Las Vegas and entered a casino. One Martian noticed a row of slot machines and called to the others: "Hey, look, fellows, slot machines."

♂    ♂    ♂

A rich Texan saw a space ship on the street and said he'd pay any price to get it. The owner said: "$750,000." "Sold," cried the Texan. After the transaction was completed, the seller chortled to a friend: "Wait till he finds out it's last year's model."

♉    ♉    ♉

The two bopsters had saved their money and had finally saved enough to go on a tourist flight through space. "Hey, dad," said one, as they passed by the rings of Saturn. "Dig those crazy hula hoops!"

♭    ♭    ♭

A Martian received a radio message asking that he come to Earth for a television interview. The Martian wired back: "I'll be there. Too bad you can't make it up to my place sometime."

A Martian landed his space ship in Central Park. For security reasons he was hustled off to jail. "Can you read or write?" asked the police lieutenant. "Can write. No read," responded the Martian. "All right then, write your name." The Martian scrawled huge strange markings across a page. "Now what does that say?" demanded the lieutenant. "Don't know," replied the Martian, "can write. No read."

♂     ♂     ♂

The Indian and his son were standing on a hill, looking over the valley. The father said, "Some day, we Indians shall get this land back. The palefaces will go to the Moon."

☺     ☺     ☺

An astronaut was rocketed five thousand miles straight into the heavens. When he reached the zenith and was about to descend, he was instructed to look out a porthole and observe the Earth. He saw a small green ball rotating, and with great awe and emotion uttered "Oh, my God." A voice beside him said: "Yes?"

**12**

A Martian walked into a bar and ordered a martini. "That'll be two dollars," said the bartender, and then
added: "You're the first Martian I've
seen around here." "At two dollars a
drink," the Martian snorted, "it's no
wonder."

Travel has always been a pleasure; now it is *out of this world!*

The girl on Earth telephoned her mother that she had just gotten married.

"Wonderful," enthused the mother.

"But mother, my husband is a Martian," said the daughter.

"Well, everybody can't be from Earth," replied the mother.

"We have no place to stay," complained the younger woman. "When landlords look at my husband, they refuse to rent to us."

"You and your husband come right over and stay here," said the doting mother.

The daughter, puzzled, asked, "But where, mother? You don't have room."

The mother said, "You and your husband can stay in our bedroom. Daddy will stay on the sofa."

"You're so nice to us, mother, but where will you sleep?"

The mother replied, "Don't worry about me, dear. As soon as I hang up, I'm going to drop dead."

The delivery truck shot down the street and made a sharp right turn. A package fell out of the truck. A visitor from Mercury chased the truck up the street, yelling, "Hey, lady, hey, you dropped your purse!"

☿　　☿　　☿

The space ship approached the Earth, and the two Martians leaned excitedly over the edge of their chairs. They approached the Mount Palomar observatory, where they saw the lens of the giant telescope. "He's in there!" said the older Martian. "I'd recognize that eye anywhere."

♂　　♂　　♂

The traveler from Pluto was very impressed with the new giant office building that had just been completed. It had fully automatic elevators. The Plutonian entered the elevator and rode up to the top floor. He watched as the lights flickered from one floor number to another during his ascent, marking his progress. He said to the elevator, "I like your style, young fellow. You've got a nice smile. How long are you in for?"

The man from Pluto was sitting on the curb rocking his head from side to side like a pendulum. A group of pedestrians had gathered and was watching the strange sight. One member of the group had the courage to ask the creature what he was doing.

"Telling the time," was his reply.

"Well then, what time is it?"

"6:15."

"No, I believe you're wrong," corrected the Earthling. "It's exactly 6:45."

"It is!" exclaimed the Plutonian, moving his head faster and faster. "I must be slow!"

♀       ♀       ♀

A Venutian space ship landed in a sand trap on a golf course. The pilot radioed back to Venus asking, "What should I do now?" Swiftly came the answer: "Use a Seven Iron, stupid."

♀       ♀       ♀

A lady Martian visiting Earth noticed an apartment building roof crowded with television aerials. She called out: "Hey, kids, climb down from there before you hurt yourselves."

Two space men landed on Earth and were greeted by a movie mogul. "See," said one of the visitors, "I told you it was a waste of time to study English."

The space ship from Jupiter landed in a Texas oil field. An oil well was emitting streams of black liquid. When the ship landed, its commander summoned the physician traveling with them and said, "Doc, better take care of that guy before he bleeds to death!"

♃    ♃    ♃

A survey conducted among chorus girls to determine how familiar they were with space-age lingo yielded the following results:

13.4% defined "capsule" as a vitamin pill.

17.2% thought "jets" were shiny black beads.

26.9% connected "flare" with the skirts of their costumes.

56.7% had a doting "antenna" back home.

♉    ♉    ♉

The green men from outer space walked down a street in New York, eating the garbage cans which were awaiting collection near the curb. One of the travelers burped, and said to his compatriots, "The crusts are good, but the fillings are very rich."

**18**

The American astronauts had landed undetected on Venus, and crept to a hilltop overlooking a Venutian military training camp. They listened as the drill sergeant put his platoon through their paces. "Left, left, left, right, right, right, left, left, left...."

♀    ♀    ♀

The space craft from Mars landed on the Lower East Side of New York City. One of the tires on the vehicle blew out during the landing. In the vehicle commander's search for a new tire, he spotted a bagel in a delicatessen window. He entered the store and asked the proprietor for the tire. The proprietor explained that it was a bagel, not a tire, and was to be eaten. The Martian took a bite, savored it for a moment, and said, "This should be real good with cream cheese."

♂    ♂    ♂

The little space man had fallen into a pile of leaves. A forester began approaching the leaves, when the space man said, "Rake me to your leader!"

Several space men were seated in a restaurant, after a long voyage from a distant planet. They were hungry after the trip, and one of them began munching on a pepper grinder that was on the table. "How is it?" asked one. "Not too bad," was the reply. "But it could use some salt."

♈     ♈     ♈

The two Venutians strolled over to a car rental agency, and asked the clerk for a Ford, "What year?" inquired the clerk. "1979," replied the older Venutian.

♀     ♀     ♀

The Martian was lying on the psychiatrist's couch, complaining of his migraine headaches. "Well," said the doctor, "I'll have to send you to a specialist in psychosomatic medicine for a valve job."

♂     ♂     ♂

Soon after the United States launched its Explorer satellite, the radio receiver at our leading observatory picked up a signal that was being sent from Explorer to Sputnik, *"Wie geht's?"*

A young man was asked why he had not applied for the opportunity of going on the next space shot, since he seemed to have all the necessary qualifications. "I like a job where you have some security and feel that you can get ahead," he said. "Look at a fellow like Colonel Glenn. He went up only once, and never again. There's no advancement in that job."

☿ ☿ ☿

A Martian landed in Reno and walked by a slot machine. At that moment the machine whirred noisily and then hit the jackpot. Coins came jangling out. Turning to the machine, the Martian said: "You shouldn't be out with a cold like that."

♂ ♂ ♂

There was much discussion on why all the astronauts are married men. "It doesn't seem fair to send a married man on such a dangerous trip," said one man. "On the contrary," said his friend, "only married men should go, single men have something to live for."

The rich Texan was helping his son with his homework, which dealt with astronomy. "Some day, Daddy," said the boy, "I'd like to go to the Moon." "Don't worry, son," reassuringly advised his father, "we'll send for it tomorrow."

☺     ☺     ☺

Three travelers from Saturn arrived on Earth late for a meeting. Their leader said, "We're terribly sorry to be so late, but you know how it is at the Christmas season. We got behind some reindeer and it was stop and go traffic all the way."

♮     ♮     ♮

The man from Jupiter chanced upon a roller towel dispenser. He looked around, embarrassed, and whispered to the dispenser, "Madam, your slip is showing."

♃     ♃     ♃

The Venutians were poised over New York in their space craft. One looked down, pointed to the city, and said, "Dig that crazy space station."

Two Martians arrive at a fashionable night club and ask the doorman if he has a table for two. The doorman says to the taller Martian, "You need a tie to get in here." He goes back to his space ship and puts on his tie, and they return to the night club. The doorman asks, "What about your friend?" "That's my wife," was the reply.

♂    ♂    ♂

The visitor from Pluto had landed his space craft on Earth and was exploring the streets of a good-sized American city. In his eagerness to see the city, he had neglected to take along his special food, and had left it in the craft. After a long walk, he came to a hardware store. "Ah," he said. "Finally a restaurant."

♀    ♀    ♀

The salesman in the used rocket lot was extolling the virtues of a vehicle: "This one was owned by a retired school-teacher who never drove over seven thousand miles an hour, and only drove on Sunday."

Two astronomers were watching Mars from the observatory. Suddenly the planet disintegrated with a cataclysmic explosion. A huge mushroom cloud billowed out in space. One astronomer turned to the other and said: "See, I told you Mars has intelligent life."

Some potential astronauts were deterred from applying for the job because they felt that they could not make much money at it. "Even if they pay you $10 an hour, the whole flight may last only fifteen minutes, and you can figure out how little money that is," observed one man who had decided not to apply.

❀　　❀　　❀

The space man landed outside the Waldorf-Astoria hotel in New York, and backed up to see the doorman decked out in a multi-colored and resplendent uniform. "I don't want to see your leader," he said. Take me to your tailor instead."

♅　　♅　　♅

A Martian heard sounds of a fight and ran over to see a bully trying to knock down a parking meter. He ran toward the scene, and shouted at the bully, who ran away. The Martian fed coins into the meter, saying, "You'll come to in a minute." The meter groggily said, "I didn't talk, I kept my mouth shut."

A Martian began hugging and kissing a traffic signal. Suddenly the signal changed from "go" to "stop." Annoyed, the Martian snapped:"Just as I thought, American women are all teases."

♂ ♂ ♂

The two explorers were looking over the first roll of film developed after Tyros, the satellite with a high speed camera in its nose, had gone aloft. "I've never seen Southeast Asia looking so well," said one.

♉ ♉ ♉

An American astronaut was complaining about the difficulties of his job. "It's very lonely," he noted sadly. "You can't even talk to yourself. You go one hundred and thirty times the speed of sound. By the time you say it, you've gone so far that you can't even hear it."

♂ ♂ ♂

The Venutians were pleased to visit a tool and die plant. "I always wanted to see how babies were made," said one.

The man from outer space landed on Earth, but saw no sign of life. Walking up a hill, he noticed a man and woman, nude, sitting on the ground with the man about to bite into an apple. "No, no, no," shouted the space man. "No, for heaven's sake."

☿　　☿　　☿

The interviewer asked the astronaut what he expected to do during those lonely hours when he would be hurtling toward the faraway planets. "I plan to cry a lot," he said.

☉　　☉　　☉

The two Saturnians met on the avenue on Easter Sunday. "Dear, your space helmet looks just lovely," said one to the other.

♭　　♭　　♭

The two Martians were walking along the street, when they observed a motor scooter parked on the street. They walked over to the scooter, and one asked, "What's a young kid like you doing out so late, by yourself?"

The couple from Venus was sitting down to dinner. "Oh damn, Trudy! Hub caps again for dinner! Pass the catsup and I'll try to make them edible."

♀     ♀     ♀

The visitors from Neptune were very impressed with the American supermarket they were visiting. One said, "Let's find out where the food is." His friend went over to a clerk, and said, "Take me to your Liederkranz."

♆     ♆     ♆

The space ship from Pluto had crash landed. "We'll never get back home," wailed the Plutonian. He looked at his co-pilot, who seemed dazed. "Come on now, let's think this through together. Four heads are better than two!"

♇     ♇     ♇

During the Eisenhower administration, a Martian landed on the White House lawn, wearing a snappy vicuna coat. "Lead me to your taker," he said to the Secret Service guard.

The visitors from Uranus landed in downtown New York. One said, "These buildings are dizzying. When I get back, I'm going to need treatment for an edifice complex."

♅     ♅     ♅

A visitor from Jupiter noticed an irate father whipping his son. The son was spread over the father's knees, and was crying. The space man shook his head and said, "I don't like the music but I sure like that rhythm."

♃     ♃     ♃

The space ship from Saturn had landed in the desert. The commander of the vehicle approached a tall cactus plant, "We need another member for our crew," he said to the plant. "Do you want to join us?"

♄     ♄     ♄

The Martians were watching a television western in which all the characters were wearing coonskin caps. "And this is the New Frontier?" asked one.

An unemployed astronaut went to collect his unemployment insurance. He was asked if he had been fired from his previous job. "No," he said. "I was fired into the job."

☿        ☿        ☿

Some skeptics were questioning whether being selected to be an astronaut was really such a distinction after all. "How good a job can it be?" asked one. "If it were really a good job, the President would give it to his brother or brother-in-law."

♃        ♃        ♃

The travelers from the Moon landed in a suburban development and took cover. One crawled over to a rotating clothes line in the back yard and whispered, "Will you help us?"

☺        ☺        ☺

Two men who were close friends in Budapest met on Mars. "Well," said one happily, "isn't the universe small?" "No," said the other, "Budapest is big."

The four visitors from Neptune were dressed to the nines in their space suits, and walked by a policeman, who began laughing uproariously at the sight of the visitors. One Neptunian turned and said to his colleague, "We frightened him silly."

♆    ♆    ♆

The Venutian landed his space craft near a small town on a Saturday night and was attracted to the local tavern. He looked the juke box square in its flashing, jangling, spinning face and asked, "What's a slick chick like you doing in a dead burg like this?"

♀    ♀    ♀

A streamlined flying saucer deposited a dozen Martians on Broadway, the electric bulbs atop their heads flashing with excitement. Their leader marched unhesitatingly to a fire hydrant and demanded, "Are you the boss around here?" His aide, however, pulled him back. "What do you want to bother with him for, chief?" he grumbled. "Can't you see he's only a kid?"

The man in the Moon noticed Sputnik
scooting by very rapidly, and asked,
"Hey, little fella, what's your hurry?

I go around the Earth only every twenty-eight days or so." Sputnik replied, "Yes, but you're not trying to get away from the Russians."

☺   ☺   ☺

The Martian and his wife were passing a hardware store when she stopped to look at the paints in the window. "I'm sorry," said the man. "Your old coat will just have to last another season."

♂   ♂   ♂

Although the Russian cosmonaut was said to be in ideal physical, emotional, and psychological health, some Russians were sure that there must be something seriously wrong with him: "What can you say about a man who goes completely around the world so many times, and lands right back in the Soviet Union?"

☿   ☿   ☿

The Martian walked unhesitatingly up to the piano in the concert hall, and said, "Take me to your dentist!"

**33**

The Martians craned their necks to see the Earth as their rocket ship sped toward it. The ship landed on a main shopping street, that was studded with parking meters. One of the Martians pointed to the meters: "Look, fellows, dames!"

The Martians ran toward the meters, each embracing the object of his affections. Only one meter was left alone.

"Wait for me," called a voice from the rocket ship. The last Martian stumbled out of the ship and embraced and kissed the one remaining meter. He noticed his colleagues were laughing at him. "What's so funny?" he asked belligerently.

"Hah, hah," they laughed, "you got the ugly one!"

☌　　☌　　☌

The American astronauts had established contact with Mercury, and had been invited to visit it. Elaborate arrangements had been made for the trip, via interplanetary radio. An official welcome and tour of the capital of Mercury had been arranged. The first stop on the hour, once the Americans had washed up and been given the keys to the planet, was a baby factory. The Americans were astounded to see that the factory was similar to a Detroit automobile factory.

When the tour was over, one of the Astronauts could no longer restrain himself. "That certainly isn't how we make babies on Earth," he told the guide.

"Is that so?" asked the Mercury guide. "How do you do it?"

The astronaut gave a detailed explanation.

"Well, how about that!" whistled the guide. "That's just the way we make automobiles up here!"

☿     ☿     ☿

Several visitors to the Cape Canaveral rocket center came to the office of the astronaut who was scheduled to go around the Earth the following Tuesday. No one answered their knock on the door, and they were nonplussed until one of the visitors pointed to a small sign over the door: "Out to launch."

The newly arrived travelers from Jupiter were sitting in the furnished apartment they had rented. They had just finished making some coffee in an electric percolator, the "Ready" light on which was flashing regularly. Both men were leering at the percolator. "I saw her first," said one. "So what," argued the other. "She winked at *me!*"

♃    ♃    ♃

The Venutian with five arms walked into a barber shop and approached the pretty manicurist. "Honey, could you give me a manicure?" She said, "Well, I guess so, but I'll have to charge you at least double, or maybe triple." The Venutian complained: "I can't see why. That motto on the wall there says, 'Many hands make light work.'"

♀    ♀    ♀

The men from space were in a bar, bracing themselves for the trip back to their asteroid. One asked the bartender for another round of drinks for the group. "Not for you, Terry," firmly said the leader. "You're flying tonight."

The space team that had arrived from Pluto was happily shopping in a supermarket, and had brought its cart to the checkout counter. They unloaded ten cans of Drano, two dozen light bulbs, ten flashlight batteries, and three boxes of Brillo. "Are you sure that's all you want?" asked the clerk as she rang up the last item. "Yes, that will do it," replied the leader of the Plutonians. "We're just sending some treats home to the kids."

A space ship from the Moon landed at the rim of the Grand Canyon. The man from the Moon called out, "Hello!" His echo answered, "Hello!" He said, "I'm from outer space." His echo answered, "I'm from outer space." The space man continued, "I'm from the Moon." "Don't kid me!" came the response, "everybody knows there's no life on the Moon."

Two space men hailed a taxi in a large American city. "Which way?" asked the driver. "Up," they replied in unison.

The space ship came gently to earth in the Congo, and the little green man climbed out. "Take me to your leader," he commanded the first inhabitant that he met.

"Kasavubu, Mobuto, or Lumumba?" she inquired.

"Never mind that now," snapped the little green man. "I wish to be taken to your leader immediately! We can dance later."

♀　　♀　　♀

The travelers from Mars were floating down toward Earth. Through the window of the space craft, they could see the St. Patrick's Day parade on Fifth Avenue in New York, with the paraders straddling the broad green line that ran down the center of the Avenue. "Damn!" said the craft commander. "The Venutians must have gotten here first."

♂　　♂　　♂

The photographs that the photographic satellite took of the Earth did not come out, because Brazil moved.

The chubby little man from Mercury approached the ticket window of the lobby of the theater where a hit musical was playing. His antennae were barely visible over the change ledge. "Do you have a seat in the rear?" he asked nervously.

With a sympathetic smile, the cashier said, "Of course, dear. We're very much alike underneath!"

☿      ☿      ☿

The first cosmonaut to reach the Moon is going to hope fervently that the creatures up there consider him friendly, delightful and interesting — almost anything but delicious!

☺      ☺      ☺

The Venutian couple was going to a wedding. The wife, who was somewhat uneasy about whether she was dressed properly, decided to peek at the costumes worn by other guests. She came back, crestfallen, to her husband: "The wedding is formal — everybody is wearing white antennae."

The visiting scientist from Jupiter spoke to a woman's club in America on life on Jupiter. He stressed how similar life on Earth and Jupiter really was. One lady came out after the lecture to shake his hand, which he extended enthusiastically to her. The scientist said, "Yes, we really are so much alike. The only difference is in how we make love. And I did enjoy that so much," he sighed contentedly as he disengaged his hand from hers.

♃     ♃     ♃

The Moon men had landed their space craft in front of a laundromat. They walked in and observed the clothes churning behind the small windows in the machines. One Moon man said, "It must be the diet on Earth. Every single one of these Earth people wears glasses."

☺     ☺     ☺

The Martian had come to earth in a meadow near a nudist colony. He went over to the first nudist he saw, and said, "Take me to your tailor."

A space ship landed in Manhattan; a
space man emerged and asked a passer-
by: "How do I get to Carnegie Hall?"
"Practice, my boy, practice," came the
answer.

The two sixth graders were watching a space shot launching on television. "10-9-8-7-6-5-4-3-2-1-," went the countdown. The device blasted off, went up in the air for a few hundred feet, and collapsed into the ocean. "No wonder it didn't go off," commented one young scholar to the other. "They don't even know how to count from 1 to 10."

◉    ◉    ◉

"Nice of that father to let his kid slide down his back," commented the visitor from Venus as he saw a youngster going down a sliding pond in the playground.

♀    ♀    ♀

The man from Neptune bought a dozen light bulbs in the department store. As the clerk was about to wrap them, the customer said, "Don't bother with a bag. I'll eat them here."

♆    ♆    ♆

The man from Mars approached the grand piano in a gingerly way. "Stop laughing at me," he said.

The travelers from Jupiter landed near a suburban housing development in the middle of winter, and around 6 a.m. They saw the full milk bottles outside the kitchen door of many of the buildings, and one said, "Those Earth people are really unkind to children. Imagine leaving kids out so late and in such bad weather!"

♃    ♃    ♃

A Martian noticed a customer putting two quarters in an ice-making machine on a city corner. Several dozen ice cubes rattled through the machine and came out the slot at the bottom of the machine. After the customer had picked up his ice and left, the Martian went over and asked the machine, "When do you get off work, honey?"

♂    ♂    ♂

The Earth scientist had just been introduced to a visitor from Venus at a party. "That is a beautiful plaid you have on," commented the scientist. "I had heard you Venutians were all nudists." "We are," was the reply.

The man from Neptune had landed near the nudist colony and decided to stay there for a while. He noticed that one of the nudists had a knee length beard, although all the others were clean shaven. "How come?" the man from Neptune inquired. "Well," said the bearded one, "someone has to go out for coffee."

♆        ♆        ♆

"Full Earth tonight, dear," whispered the Moon man to his sweetheart. "Look!"

☽        ☽        ☽

The visitors from Mercury were strolling in the park and came across a bubbling water fountain. "Let's get out of here," said one. "I can't stand to see a woman cry like that."

☿        ☿        ☿

Several New Yorkers were discussing how difficult it was to recognize a female Martian and tell her apart from a male. "Easy," said one. "The girls are the ones with a henna antenna."

The government of Pluto was very worried about the possibility of there being intelligent life on Earth, and about the possibility of an invasion from Earth to conquer Pluto. After many years of work, a space craft was sent to Earth to discover what was the situation with respect to the possibility of an invasion. The Plutonians landed their craft on a California freeway, near some self-service gasoline pumps. After studying the terrain, they returned to Pluto. "Don't worry about those fellows on Earth," they told their president. "They just stand around with their finger in their ears."

♀    ♀    ♀

The space headquarters on Jupiter received a radio message from its mission to Earth: "Jupiter money no good here. What shall I do?" Back came the reply: "Live economically."

♃    ♃    ♃

The Martian mother was admonishing her child: "Junior, for heaven's sake, straighten up your posture—and please take your feet out of your pockets!"

The Russian scientists selecting a cosmonaut for a trip to the Moon have had great difficulties in making a final selection, because there were so many volunteers who were eager to leave Russia for the Moon.

The two men from Mercury were discussing some of the films and television programs they had seen since arriving on Earth. "My wife has a crush on this fellow Yul Brynner," complained one. "Don't worry, it'll wear off," counseled the other. "I doubt it," replied his friend. "She's already insisted that I shave off my antennae."

☿     ☿     ☿

A Martian lady went to a psychiatrist and said, "I'm worried about my husband. He thinks he's a cowboy." "When can you bring him in?" asked the doctor. "Just as soon as he gets back from Eagles Pass."

♂     ♂     ♂

A visitor from Saturn was ambling along the main street of an American city when he was accosted by a panhandler. "Can you spare a dime?" asked the panhandler. "What's a dime?" asked the Saturnian. "You're right!" replied the beggar. "Make it a quarter."

♄     ♄     ♄

The small boy shouted, "Flying sorcerers!" as he saw some Hallowe'en witches zooming through the sky.

**49**

An American astronaut was poised in his capsule, ready to be launched. A reporter asked, "How do you feel?" "How would you feel," the astronaut replied, "if you were sitting on top of 150,000 parts, each made by the lowest bidder?"

♈        ♈        ♈

The man from Mercury walked up to the clerk in the bookstore and said, in a firm and ringing voice, "Take me to Lolita!"

☿        ☿        ☿

The Martian promised a cowboy who had captured him that any three wishes of the cowboy would be fulfilled if he let the Martian go. "Make me as rich as Rockefeller, handsome as Rock Hudson, and virile as my horse," said the cowboy. "Tomorrow," said the Martian, "my magic will work." The next morning, the cowboy awoke to find bags of gold in his room. His face no longer had any wrinkles. He began singing "Home On the Range," but heard a pure lyric soprano come out of his mouth. "Damn!" he muttered in falsetto. "I forgot I was ridin' Old Nell."

The space scientist asked the giant computer: "Is there a God?" The machine whirred, then answered: "There is now."

♈   ♈   ♈

The visitors from Pluto had finished their meal at the restaurant and been presented with the check by the waiter. They gave a large piece of uranium to the waiter, saying, "We don't have anything smaller. Could you please make change?"

♇   ♇   ♇

The traveler from Jupiter wandered into the banquet hall of the large hotel. The table was set for a formal dinner. Looking at the glowing candelabra on the table, he shook his head despairingly and said, "Tsk, tsk, you kids are too young to smoke!"

♃   ♃   ♃

A Martian doctor was clanking along a city street, when he saw an open manhole. He peered over the edge and said, "Now, say 'Ah'!"

The visiting Martian was being X-rayed by a group of distinguished American medical specialists. The physicians were astonished at the complexity of the structure revealed by the X-ray. "Remarkable," said one. "Those Martians are run by machines. And what complicated machines! Look at that network of interlocking gears!"

"Wait a minute," the specialist said, "what is that over there? It looks like writing on one of the wheels. It is writing! I believe I can make it out . . . M-A-D-E-I-N-J-A-P-A-N . . ."

♂        ♂        ♂

The visitor from Mercury walked into the music store, nodded pleasantly at the sales clerk, and requested, "Take me to your *Lieder*."

☿        ☿        ☿

The two men on the Moon were talking on a street corner. A dog began barking excitedly a few feet away. One of the Moon men pointed to the Earth and said, "There's always something eerie about a dog barking at the Earth."

Two Martians with antennae sticking out from their heads walked into a restaurant. The hat check girl asked: "Check your hats, gentlemen?" "No thanks, we're expecting a call."

A Martian observed a man inserting a coin in a cigarette vending machine and pressing a button. The machine whirred, but no cigarettes came out. The man punched the machine excitedly and vigorously, and left. The Martian approached the machine and asked, "Does it hurt?" "No," the machine replied. "Only when it's Camels."

♂     ♂     ♂

Two matrons from Mercury were taking a vacation on Earth. They wandered past an automobile junk yard, crammed with rusting parts and automobiles. "Look, Laura," squealed one, pointing to the tons of metal. "Now, Evelyn," scolded her friend, "a vacation is not an excuse to stuff yourself with sweets!"

☿     ☿     ☿

The Venutian was sitting in a sidewalk café in Greenwich Village. He drank one glass of wine after another. Finally he looked affectionately at the glass on the table before him, and whispered, "Take me to your litre."

**54**

The visitors from Venus had gone to a state fair in order to get a feeling for American life. They saw a man looking through a sidewalk telescope, just at the moment that a falling star shot across the sky. "Will you look at that, Timothy," said one Venutian to the other. "Those Americans are really crack shots, aren't they?"

♀ ♀ ♀

The picture-taking satellite should be of great help to weather forecasts. They'll still be unable to predict weather accurately but they will have all the data they need.

☉ ☉ ☉

A huge crowd of people watched the little green man from space as he calmly walked through Grand Central Station. He walked down the stairs and disappeared through the door of the men's room. The onlookers waited for him to appear, almost breathless with anticipation. After a short time, he poked his head out the door and asked, "Anyone got change for a quarter?"

Two Martians landed on Earth and consented to a television interview. "Can you tell me your age?" asked the interviewer. "I'm three hundred years old," the Martian responded. Turning to the other Martian, the interviewer asked with obvious disbelief: "Do you really think he's that old?" "I can't say for certain. I've only flown with him for one hundred years."

♂      ♂      ♂

The man from Mercury was cramped and uncomfortable in his tiny space ship as it hurtled to Earth. He maneuvered his vehicle to a halt in a wheat field, and rushed over to a speechless farmer. "Please, please, please," he shouted to the farmer, "take me to your men's room!"

☿      ☿      ☿

The men from the Moon were being shown through an American astronomer's observatory. They looked at the Moon through the telescope. "You'd never guess, looking at it from here, that it was made of green cheese," commented one of the Moon men.

One reason the French are having so much trouble with their atomic bomb tests is that their bombs don't explode — they pop.

☉      ☉      ☉

The Venutian had come to Las Vegas and had chanced on two slot machines. One was fairly large and the other was much smaller. Both machines had three plums showing in each of their little glass windows. Patting the smaller machine affectionately, he said, "You're a handsome little boy, sonny, and you certainly have your mother's eyes."

♀      ♀      ♀

The Martian lands his space ship near Times Square, walks over to the Actors' Studio, and confronts the Studio's artistic director, Lee Strasberg. "Take me to your leader," the Martian says. "Not bad at all," replied Strasberg. "But try it once more, with less tension. Try to feel yourself in the part, and let your own natural colors as an actor come through. All right, now, whenever you're ready . . ."

**57**

The Saturn Academy of Science had sent a mission to Earth to study whether the Saturnian race might be strengthened by cross-breeding with Earth people. The first thing the Saturnian saw on Earth was a barber pole, to which he said, "Take me to your leader." When he received no reply, he flew back to Saturn in disgust. "These Earth people sure are dumb," he told the Academy. "But what a blood stream!"

♄    ♄    ♄

The man from Uranus was describing his domestic difficulties to a friend. "My wife wants me to give her ten batteries a week for alimony," he complained. "But I can only afford to give her eight batteries."

♁    ♁    ♁

The teacher had asked the class to count backwards to ten. Sidney had volunteered to do so. "Ten, nine, eight, seven, six, five, four, three — oh, damn!" The teacher asked, "Why do you swear? You were doing fine." Sidney replied, "That's how my dad does it, and he works at Cape Canaveral."

Two Martians entered a restaurant and sat down at a table. The place settings were all ready, and the waiter put the silverware on the table. One Martian began eating the silverware. The other said, "This must be a good restaurant. We didn't even order and they brought us what we want."

♂ ♂ ♂

The man from Saturn and his friend from Pluto were walking down Broadway, bored and looking for a movie that they could go to in order to kill time before a trip. One pointed to a marquee on the next block, and asked, "How about that?" "CHILLING SPINE-TINGLING DOUBLE BILL SCIENCE FICTION CLASSICS," read the friend. "No," he said. "What's to see? I'm sick of those documentaries."

♀ ♀ ♀

The Martian visitor was staying with an American scientist and his wife, who was famous for her tact and good sense. On the towels in the bathroom of the home was written: His — Hers — Its.

**59**

Two rats were in a nose cone shooting through space. One rat said to the other rat, "And to think we might have been in cancer research!"

The little green men were peering through their telescope at the terrain. The American scientist asked one of the men, "What are you looking for?" "Little green women, of course," snapped the man. "What do you take us for?"

♀    ♀    ♀

The visitor from Mercury was visiting an optometrist for an eye examination. "Read the sixth line down," said the doctor. "L-M-2-C-X-4-F," read the visitor. "Doctor, I don't want to offend you, but that word should be spelled with two X's."

☿    ☿    ☿

The Martian was standing at the bar, quietly sipping at his beer. He was wearing his space equipment, with wires sticking out of his costume and lights flashing. A suburban couple sat nearby, and began quarreling noisily. They became vituperative, the husband walked out alone angrily, and the wife followed. "I guess it takes all kinds to make a world," said the Martian philosophically to the bartender.

The group of visitors from Pluto was strolling down a street in the middle of a shopping center. One observed an unclothed mannequin in a window. He pointed to the mannequin, threw himself to his knees, and cried, "Look, fellows, our leader!"

♀      ♀      ♀

Many camera fans wondered who changed the film in those satellite cameras.

☉      ☉      ☉

A Martian was bragging about his girl friend to a friend: "That Univac gal is not only beautiful, but she's got brains as well."

♂      ♂      ♂

The wife of a visiting Martian was expecting. She was taken to a hospital and the bewildered obstetricians went to work with hack saws, screwdrivers, and chisels. The delivery was a success, and the nurse took the child out on its wobbly little wheels to see its father. "Congratulations," she exclaimed, "it's a toy!"

**62**